MOODS OF
WORCESTERSHIRE
& ELGAR COUNTRY

VAN GREAVES

HALSGROVE

First published in Great Britain in 2005

Frontispiece photograph: **From Pinnacle Hill, southwards along the Malverns**

British Library Cataloguing-in-Publication Data
A CIP record for this title is available from the British Library

ISBN 1 84114 466 5

HALSGROVE
Halsgrove House
Lower Moor Way
Tiverton, Devon EX16 6SS
Tel: 01884 243242
Fax: 01884 243325
email: sales@halsgrove.com
website: www.halsgrove.com

Printed and bound by D'Auria Industrie Grafiche Spa, Italy

INTRODUCTION

Quintessentially England, Worcestershire is by and large a rural county. Beautiful rolling hills encompass its north eastern, northern, western and southern boundaries, the most impressive of which are the geologically-ancient Malverns, which rise abruptly from the Severn Plain and provide a serrated skyline from almost any angle.

Edward Elgar (1857-1934), one of England's finest composers, gleaned much of his inspiration from these surroundings. His inconspicuous cottage birthplace with pretty garden still stands in Lower Broadheath, and is now a museum to his life and works.

The long elevated ridge of northern hills culminates in the Clent Hills, bounding Birmingham and the Black Country on one side and giving endless rural vistas to the west. The North Worcestershire long distance footpath goes from Major's Green adjacent to the suburb of Shirley for 27 miles across these hills to gentler country culminating in Kingsford Country Park (and Kinver Edge), under which a beautiful bowl of birch woodland lies where it meets the Staffordshire and Worcestershire Ways.

West of here, a lateral ridge guards the sylvan Severn Valley, dominated by the Wyre Forest, and threaded by the famous river and a vintage steam railway line. The Worcestershire Way follows this over many undulations beyond Bewdley, a classic Georgian town, until a fine line of hills meets the sequestered Teme Valley to eventually reach the Malverns.

The Vale of Evesham and the Midlands Avon makes up the central plain of fields and lanes interspersed by historic villages, backed in the south by Bredon Hill where Cotswold stone infiltrates Worcestershire, leading to Broadway.

Worcester itself has enough historic sites, including the marvellous cathedral, to fill its own book. Elsewhere, think (historically) of carpets from Kidderminster, needles from Redditch, salt from Droitwich, and the historic towns of Pershore and Evesham. The incredible diversity of Worcestershire and Elgar Country, shown here in these photographs, should speak for itself.

Van Greaves

LOCATION MAP

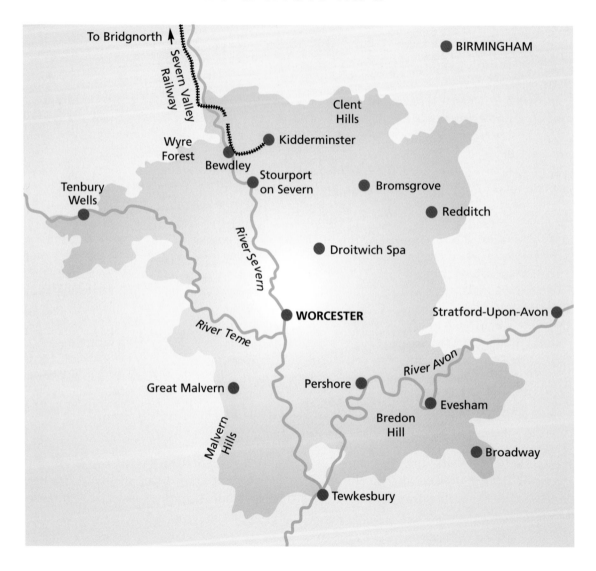

Christmas: High Street Precinct and Worcester Cathedral
This photograph was taken outside a modern department store which stands
on the site of the former Elgar family music shop, now sadly disappeared.

Dawnscape, Bredon Hill
An early ascent of Bredon Hill in December was rewarded by this moody shot.
The mists swirl across the hillside, and the distant Malvern Hills are crowned by pre-sunrise pink light.

Worcestershire Beacon, Winter
Even in these times of climate change, there are still occasions when snow covers the Malvern Hills.
This view shows the crowning summit of Worcestershire Beacon (1395ft/425m), as seen from North Hill.

Near Dowles Brook, Wyre Forest
Wyre Forest, a National Nature Reserve, is one of the three largest natural forests left in England.
It is a haven for wildlife, fungi and plants, and numerous walks thread through the trees.

Autumn at Hurcott Pool
The hamlet of Hurcott is situated on the east side of Kidderminster.
It supports woods and pools which are frequented mainly by local people.

Elgar's Birthplace, Lower Broadheath
A simple cottage and garden at
Lower Broadheath mark the birthplace
of one of England's greatest composers.
You can visit it along with the adjacent
museum dedicated to the great man.

Cottage, Teme Valley
Careful exploration of the beautiful Teme Valley revealed this lovely isolated cottage, seen here in autumn.
I have several images of this, but chose this one for its spotlight effect.

Scene in Broadway

Broadway is often known as 'The gateway to the Cotswolds', where the county boundary intrudes into Cotswold country. Broadway is a well-known tourist honeypot, which can be crowded in the height of summer.

Pump Rooms, Tenbury Wells

The Pump Rooms at the former spa town of Tenby Wells were originally built in 1862. They have had a chequered history of neglect and restoration, and the most recent renovations were completed in 1998.

River Severn from the Stourport Steamer
River trips are popular out of Stourport, so I took one to obtain this unusual picture.

Whitford Bridge, on the Birmingham-Worcester Canal
Another form of water travel has been preserved, primarily for tourism,
on this most picturesque of canals, seen here near Stoke Prior.

Frosty pickings
Two horses in unison are seen on Romsley Hill, with Walton Hill peeping out of the fog beyond.

Sheep and Clent Hills
I saw these clouds one evening from my back garden. I dashed out and luckily found this field
with sheep with the Clent Hills as a backdrop. I have learned over the years to attract the attention
of sheep rather than frighten them off, and this has resulted in some intriguing images.

Spetchley Park
Early spring creates an attractive view of this stately home and landscaped
grounds open to the public, just across the M5 to the east of Worcester.

Cropthorne Mill and the River Avon
This is a picturesque spot between Fladbury and Cropthorne.

Birtsmorton Court
This moated property, only open one or two times a year, lies beneath the Malvern Hills, and stands in its own landscaped gardens.

Westwood House, near Droitwich
Unless you are walking the Wychavon Way, you might never know of this fine
Jacobean hunting lodge, set well beyond view of the nearest road. I only discovered
it by having a client who lived in an adjacent building on the estate.

We'll meet again... Kidderminster Station
Every year on two weekends in July, there is a 1940s weekend all along the stations
of the Severn Valley Railway. This photograph captures the spirit of the occasion.

Sea Lion Pool, West Midlands Safari Park
Crowds gather for the afternoon shows at this popular venue,
especially when the sea lions are fed in return for showing off their talents.

Stone Cottage Garden
A visit to this privately-owned garden and nursery near Kidderminster is well worth while in spring and summer.

Severn-side autumn, Arley Arboretum
Rich colours from the changing leaves provide a highly-pictorial composition. Visitors enjoy the beauty of a Severn-side autumn.

Horse Guards at Three Counties Show, Malvern
The three-day Three Counties Show, held in the shadow of the Malvern Hills at Great Malvern every June,
is an important date in the county's social calendar. Here the Horse Guards give their colourful display.

Judging the Gun Dogs at the Three Counties Show, Malvern

First Light on Pershore from Bredon Hill
Another image in the lovely set I obtained from my December dawn visit.

Hawthorn on Bredon Hill
The hawthorn berries linger well into December on the twisted trees on
the scarp slope edge of Bredon Hill. The village below is Great Comberton.

Severn floods – sundown at Severnstoke
The water seen in the bottom half of the picture completely inundates acres of low-lying fields when the River Severn bursts its banks after heavy rains. Its stillness and the reflective sky make a striking image.

Rainbow and Clent Hills
Photographing rainbows is an elusive exercise. You can't be choosy with your foregrounds. You either take them or not, for they are gone all too quickly. After a severe thunderstorm, this is the sight which greeted me on returning home above Wolverley.

Canal and St Augustine's Church, Droitwich

Astley Hall, near Stourport

The former home of Stanley Baldwin, who was born in Bewdley and three times British prime minister, is now an elderly persons' residence. Strangely, little seems to be known about Baldwin's time there, although carved initials over the front porch (SLB, 1912) seem to indicate the year he bought the house.

Epitaph with snowdrops, Eastham Church, Teme Valley
I have photographed many old churches in Worcestershire, and I searched this churchyard for a meaningful picture as the snowdrops were out. It was just possible to read part of the tombstone inscription, and I found it poignant that I had already lived three times longer than this brave young soldier who laid down his life so that the likes of myself could enjoy my freedom.

Blossom groves, Vale of Evesham
As with the snowdrops in the previous picture, I required something more intimate as I chose to shoot a portion of these apple groves.

Evesham Abbey
Only the half-timbered gateway and 110-foot campanile (bell tower) of this former monastery remain.

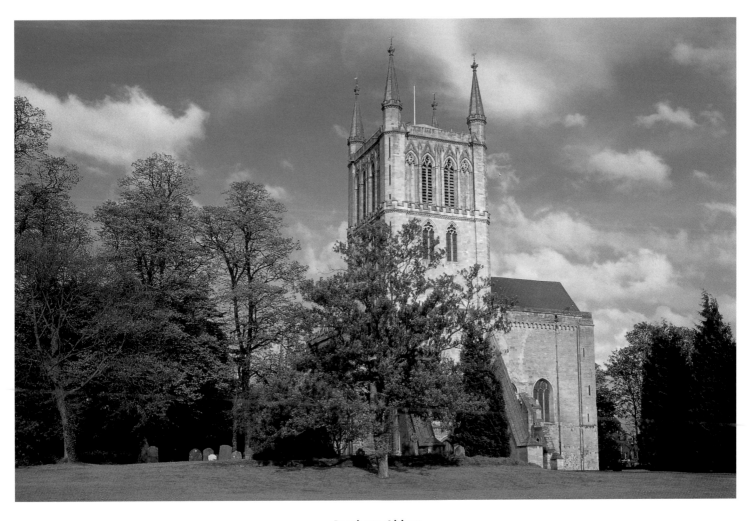

Pershore Abbey
There are some great views of this elegant church and its fourteenth-century
Cotswold-stone tower from the parkland behind the town.

Arley Station, Severn Valley Railway
The milk churns add a touch of nostalgia to this beautiful location, a favourite stop for travellers on the restored Severn Valley Railway.

Kidderminster Station, Severn Valley Railway
Summer visitors enjoy the weather on the platform of this preserved Great Western station, as a locomotive approaches.

Hanbury Church
Hanbury parish church is a prominent building in the village which lies on a minor road to the south of Bromsgrove.

Rock Church
The wonderful twelfth century church of St Peter and St Paul at Rock, deep in the
Worcestershire countryside to the south of the Wyre Forest, is a notable landmark.
It has the largest Norman arch separating the nave from the chancel in the county.

Scarecrows at Belbroughton

Every year in this attractive village there is a scarecrow festival. The residents make the dummies, which are often positioned outside their homes with humourous notes appended.

Residents and cottage, Ashton under Hill
Two ladies pass the time of day outside a typical thatched cottage in this
village which lies sheltered, as its name suggests, under Bredon Hill.

Pool in Wyre Forest
The figures in red complement the verdant green surroundings on another walk in the forest.

Autumn over Kingsford Country Park
I cannot overstress the beauty of the autumnal birches of this area, seen here with rowan berries in the foreground.

Eastgrove Cottage Garden
This is a hidden gem of a place, near Shrawley. The owners have created
an ideal cottage garden – and they make their own ice cream too!

Garden at Menithwood
This was a private garden not open to the public, but I asked the owners if I could photograph
it and they kindly obliged. The figures add scale to what was clearly a labour of love.

Chateau Impney, Droitwich
Built as a present from John Corbett to his beautiful French governess wife in 1875, even this palatial
gift did not make the marriage last. She pined for France more than she loved him, and subsequently returned
to her homeland. These days it is a grand hotel boasting two restaurants. The grounds house farm animals.

Madresfield Court, Malvern
Now occupied by Lady Morrison, this beautiful house was originally built for the Lygon family
in the fifteenth century. It makes a compelling view when seen across the moat at its front.

Laburnum tunnel, Bodenham Arboretum
Spring heralds the appearance of this gorgeous blossom,
a stunning feature in this most picturesque of arboretums.

View from Dunley, near Stourport

Continuing with the yellow theme, these oilseed rape fields make this pleasing composition of the modern Worcestershire countryside.

Royal Worcester Porcelain – Paint Shop
Royal Worcester Porcelain is another icon of the city of Worcester. Hand painting is a hallmark
of the renowned products from this famous old factory, museum and visitor centre.

Worcestershire v. Lancashire at New Road, Worcester
Dramatic light picks out the cricketers as Worcestershire attempt to bowl out Lancashire
on a typical April day, with the cathedral brooding darkly in the background.

Romsley Hill from the North Worcestershire Path, Walton Hill
This view, enhanced by snow, of Romsley Hill from the North Worcestershire Path
at Walton Hill, has the feel of the Welsh Marches in its character.

Snow at Habberley Valley

Believe it or not, some mountaineering experience was necessary to gain this shot. Habberley Valley, near Franche, Kidderminster, begins with a pecipitous drop over a sandstone cliff, just left of the tree in the foreground.

Evening light, Broadway Tower
A gothic folly built in 1799 and standing at 1024ft (312m) on Broadway Hill,
Broadway Tower occupies the second highest summit in the Cotswold Hills.
Late December light gave the colour while the bare trees provided a graphic lead-in.

Bredon Hill and Tower to the Malverns at dawn
The Iron Age earthwork gives a colourful foreground to the BT tower on the summit, which is just short
of 1000 feet (300m) above sea level. The Malvern Hills, as ever, make an interesting background.

Hawford Dovecote
This interesting building, just off the
A449 Kidderminster to Worcester road,
is well worth an inspection.

Stained glass, Malvern Priory
The beautiful stained glass in the
Great East Window of Malvern Priory
dates from the fifteenth century, and
shows apostles and the Passion and
Resurrection. The priory has more
stained glass of this period than
any other church in Britain.

Tardebigge Church
The parish church of St Bartholomew at Tardebigge is an elegant hilltop landmark between Bromsgrove and Redditch. The slender, classical steeple is picked out here in silhouette.

Roof detail, St Michael and All Angels Church, Witley
Experience the wonderful interior to this church (dating from 1735),
with its superb frescos adorning walls and ceiling.

The Almonry, Evesham
A little cameo depicting part of this historic building, which is now used as a museum of rural life.

Cottage front, Little Comberton
Another picture in the same spirit as the previous photograph.

Pear blossom and Titterstone Clee, Teme Valley
I found this classic composition at the end of Camp Lane above Shelsley Beauchamp.

Abberley Hall Clock Tower from Walsgrove Hill
Viewed from the Worcestershire Way footpath, the daffodils add impact to the
overall scene, with the 1883 clock tower beyond, a landmark for miles around.

Severn Valley Railway, Rifle Range
The vantage point gave the curve in the line. To the right is part of the circular route around the West Midlands Safari Park.

Severn Valley Railway, Victoria Bridge
The moment is captured as the locomotive crosses this famous bridge, built by Thomas Telford, and spanning the mighty River Severn.

Huddington Court

Built in 1494, this moated house has beautiful gardens including a timber-framed dovecote, lawns and a graceful wrought-iron bridge. Originally, the site was 'the court of Hudda,' an Anglo Saxon settler. The present building was more famously the family home of the Winters, conspirators in the Gunpowder Plot of 1605.

The gardens, Huddington Court
The blossom petals floating on the moat with the white-reflected iron bridge beyond
made an ideal picture. The composition came from me, but the light was from God!

Hanbury Hall, near Droitwich
This William-and-Mary style country house was built for Thomas Vernon in 1701,
and is open to the public. It has 400 acres of parkland, with some rights of way access.

Hagley Hall, near Stourbridge
Built for the Lyttleton family in 1760, this Palladian house has fine examples of
Italian plasterwork and rich rococo decoration. It is set in 350 acres of parkland.

The Black Mountains from the Clent Hills
May days often give the clearest visibility in these parts. This view from
Walton Hill shows the distant Black Mountains with their escarpment at Hay Bluff clearly etched out.

From Walton Hill to the Black Country
Many people escape their Black Country homeland to be in the haven of the
nearby Clent Hills. The view takes in Brierley Hill, Sedgley, Dudley and Netherton.
Even the Staffordshire Moors on the edge of the Peak District can be glimpsed beyond.

A.E. Housman statue, Bromsgrove
Standing in the pedestrianised
High Street, this statue celebrates
A.E. Housman, scholar, poet, and native
of Bromsgrove, who lived between
1859 and 1936. He was a contemporary
of Elgar, whose statue is seen in the
next photograph.

Sir Edward Elgar, High Street, Worcester

Edward Elgar, (1857 to 1934), is
Worcestershire's most famous son,
and the great composer is immortalised
in Ken Pott's statue which sees him
gazing towards his beloved cathedral.
My favourite Elgar piece is 'Nimrod'
from the *Enigma Variations*. I just
dream of the Malvern Hills and
England's beauty whenever I hear it.

EDWARD ELGAR

Ragged Stone Hill from Chase End Hill
The less-frequented southern end of the Malvern Hills gives a lovely 4-mile figure of eight walk, with Hollybush as the start.
You flank the east sides of Ragged Stone Hill and Chase End Hill before returning over both tops.

Last light, Ragged Stone Hill
The outcropping rocks give an indication of how the hill obtained its name.

Bewdley
The town's abundance of Georgian buildings and St Anne's Church are etched out
in this morning view from near Crundall's Farm, on the east side of the River Severn.

River Avon, Evesham
Swans and Canada geese patrol the river in this view from the popular Abbey Park riverside path.

Stormlight near Grafton
The cows are definitely coming home as the weather threatens this period cottage under Bredon Hill.

Cottages at Elmley Castle
Note the Cotswold stone in the nearest cottage and the red brick in the
half-timbered one in this lovely village which lies under Bredon Hill.

Worcester Cathedral and the River Severn
Lush vegetation guards the riverside, as people walk the opposite bank's pathway beneath the great medieval building.

Doverdale Church
The intimacy of the wooden bell tower is captured between the boughs of a twisted tree.

The Worcestershire Way near Greenhouse Farm
This 48-mile long distance path undulates through pretty countryside, seen here in spring, between Bliss Gate and Rock.

Retrospect of Church Lench
This village, north of Evesham, stands on a small hill, and is seen
here to advantage across the foreground of a rape field.

Balloon over Pinnacle Hill, Malvern Hills
A summer evening's flight along the Malvern crest, showing Bredon Hill in the background.

Silver-washed fritillary on thistle
Thistles are a favourite plant of this butterfly, which is sometimes used as an emblem for the Wyre Forest.
Visit the forest's leafy rides on a good day in August and you may well see it flitting from flower to flower.
Its name is gained from the colour of the underside of its wings, seen here as it sucks nectar.

County Museum, Hartlebury Castle, near Stourport
This is an unusual angle of the building taken from a little known lane at its rear.

Harvington Hall, near Kidderminster
Harvington Hall is a medieval and
Elizabethan manor house perfectly
situated around a moat and pool,
from which this image was taken.

Above Kingsford Country Park
Two walkers enjoy their surroundings in excellent walking country west of the popular country park.

Upper Arley
Walkers and trippers alike enjoy the riverside village in the Severn Valley.

Upper Bittell Reservoir
Another view on the North Worcestershire Path, this is one of very few reservoirs in the county.
It is home of the Barnt Green Sailing Club.

Duckpond, Hanley Swan
Irises make a foreground across the pond to the old post office
in this village on the flats beneath the Malvern Hills.

Late autumn, towards Woodbury Hill, Teme Valley

May Hill from Bredon Hill
This dawn shot looks south-west from Bredon Hill's summit across a milky Severn Plain to the tree-topped May Hill in Gloucestershire.

Cottage fronts, Honeybourne
This and the following picture are examples of houses in villages tucked away in the south-eastern corner of the county.

Cottages in Breforton

Temperature inversion, Walton Hill to Titterstone Clee Hill
When the temperature in valleys gets lower than on hills, mists or cloud can lie low and obscure them.
This phenomenon is often reserved for higher places such as mountains, but is can also happen in Worcestershire.
The whaleback of Radnor Forest in Wales can be seen peeping out of the mist to the left of Titterstone Clee Hill.

May evening, north Worcestershire, looking towards Frankley Beeches
The balance of the cloud formation with the position of the tree
and the contrast in colours made a very pleasing picture.

Manor House Gardens, near Pershore
This venue is open on specific days under the National Gardens Scheme.

Queen Elizabeth II Jubilee Gardens, Bewdley
This is a lovely backwater of Bewdley, not obvious until a careful look along High Street reveals the entrance.

Walkers at Trimpley Reservoir
The joy of walking in beautiful surroundings is captured here in this lovely setting alongside the River Severn.

The Staffordshire and Worcestershire Canal near Wolverley
The Staffordshire and Worcestershire Canal near Wolverley provides more sylvan walking.

Acer leaves in autumn
Arley Arboretum has several of
these trees, whose changing leaves
make striking photographic subjects.

Poppy in linseed field
A couple of years ago, just off the
Bewdley bypass, I saw a field of blue
and red. I couldn't wait to visit it for this
close-up and for lengthier views.

Linseed field and poppies, towards Bewdley and Brown Clee Hill
The field gave an unusually colourful foreground to a prospect
of the town, which normally would be very hard to come by.

Great Malvern and Bredon Hill from North Hill
A snowbound scene helps etch this bird's eye view over the town and the Severn Plain, with Bredon Hill and the Cotswolds beyond.

**Below Vales Rock,
Kingsford Country Park**
This is a sandstone promontory
in this popular visitor attraction
near Kidderminster.

Blackstone Rock, near Bewdley
Surely a misnomer, for this is red sandstone! Nevertheless it is probably the biggest sheer cliff in
Worcestershire and it sits alongside the River Severn a mile out of town.

Guildhall Study, Worcester
The 1721 building by Thomas White simply exudes baroque splendour.

Greyfriars, Worcester
Another historic quarter of this fine city, now pedestrianised so it can be enjoyed more fully.

Croome Park near Pershore
Designed by Capability Brown, the 670-acre park was once described as second only to Kew
in terms of its exotic plants. The National Trust is slowly restoring the landscape to its former glories.

Perseus and Andromeda Fountain, Witley Court

Now an English Heritage site, Witley Court was originally a Jacobean manor house converted in the nineteenth century by the Earl of Dudley into a huge Italianate mansion. The restored fountain shoots 120 feet high.

By permission of English Heritage

Greater butterfly orchid
Not a rare plant, but rather localised in shady woodland, this fine example was photographed in Monk Wood, a Site of Special Scientific Interest.

Woodland beams, Chaddesley Woods
This type of photograph is on any discerning photographer's list.

Stourport
A riot of flowers decorate the town near the canal every spring.

Redditch town centre
The picture shows St Stephen's Church and Church Green.

Kyre Park, near Tenbury

Pronounced 'Keer', this venue is signposted off the Tenbury to Worcester road. It is on the site of a former Norman castle, now privately owned. Enjoy the Georgian additions of the Pytt family, and the late 1930s replacements by the Earl of Clarendon, as well as the attractive parkland.

Salwarpe Court, near Droitwich
A hidden gem of a building, unless you find the no-through lane sign-posted
to the hamlet of Salwarpe out of Droitwich, where it lies off the village green.

Tithe Barn, Middle Littleton
A rare example of a thirteenth-century tithe barn, where some of the tithes due to Evesham Abbey were held.

Norman Church, Abberley
Volunteers lovingly restored the chancel of this church in the 1960s.

Bluebell dingle, Clent Hills
To find and enjoy this type of light filtering into the wooded slopes, you must
contour round the flanks of Walton Hill on a sunny evening in spring.

Maple leaves and fir
A 'design' picture, capturing a corner of Bodenham Arboretum, near Kingsford Country Park, which is beautiful at this time of year.

Cottages at Feckenham

These fine cottages have been photographed at an angle which belies their position, facing the Droitwich to Alcester road.

Cottage at Crowle
Another careful composition where the part rather than the whole conveys the design.
Crowle village has several of these beautiful cottages.

Stourport Basin
The colourful narrow boats make a graphic image in the thin winter light.

Upstream, River Severn at Lenchford
This is the site of a popular hostelry and mooring area for boats on the river.

Typical scenery near Heightington
A successful landscape contained without a sky, but accentuated by the light on
the field patterns and a solitary tree that 'explodes' like an atom bomb.

From British Camp, looking north along the Malverns
A classic landscape where the earthworks of the hillfort give an interesting foreground, and
the ridge curves away from right to left, accentuated by dramatic light from an impending weather front.

Bredon village
An intimate look at this lovely village sited under Bredon Hill.

Ombersley
The twisted, classic Elizabethan chimney and ornate half-timbers of the house, left, determined my choice of viewpoint.

Weaver's Wharf, Kidderminster
These re-vamped carpet warehouses, now retail shops, make Kidderminster more attractive to tourists.

Marina and 'Pepperpot', Upton on Severn
A Bavarian-style cupola was added to the thirteenth-century tower, seen above
the trees cloaking the marina. Its local nickname is, inevitably, 'The Pepperpot.'

Chaddesley Corbett and the Clee Hills
The retrospect from the walk to Chaddesley Woods gives this most English of scenes.

From Crutch Hill, near Droitwich
Conical Crutch Hill is only 253ft (77m) above sea level, but it gives extensive views in all directions. This angle shows Abberley and Woodbury Hills, with the Abberley Hall clock tower visible in between them.

Great Malvern Priory
One of England's outstanding
parish churches, originally founded
as early as 1085.

Little Malvern Priory and Little Malvern Court
Seen from the adjacent right of way, the two historic buildings both lie in the shelter of the Malvern Hills.

Overbury and Overbury Court
Note the half-timbered structure on the building (left), a style of architecture which is repeated elsewhere in the village. The court is of Cotswold stone and dates from the early eighteenth century.

St Peter's Church, Croome
This is a fine example of a half-timbered church, of which there are a number in Worcestershire.

Spring scene, Crew Hill
This is essentially a Worcestershire scene, if ever there was one.
The Worcestershire Way long distance footpath crosses the skyline.

Knowles Mill, Wyre Forest
If I saw Rupert the Bear coming out of this place, I'd believe it, as it occupies a position well
into the forest, and would have used the Dowles Brook alongside for power in times gone by.

Winter scene, 'Trimpley Hills'
Seen from the opposite side to the cliff edge of Habberley Valley, there are no named 'Trimpley Hills', but as they spill off the area known as Trimpley, I gave them this name. Anyway, the early morning light on the landscape made the picture well worth including.

Rous Lench, near Evesham
As the year moves on, daffodils adorn this attractive village green near the Warwickshire border.

Scene in Clifton upon Teme
The village pump and the 'Old Smithy' are condensed into an interesting composition.